I Promise

Written and Illustrated by
Megan Wittwood

Dedicated to Lawson James

May your eyes remain curious

...

May your heart be filled with kindness

...

May your hands forever yearn to help

...

I am with you always

...

I Promise

A special thanks to Grandma Nancy. For all of your love and wisdom.
Your values and virtues have impacted me as a mother.
I hope to do the same for my son; your grandson.

I can't
PROMISE
You won't be
afraid,
When you see
shadows
in the night...

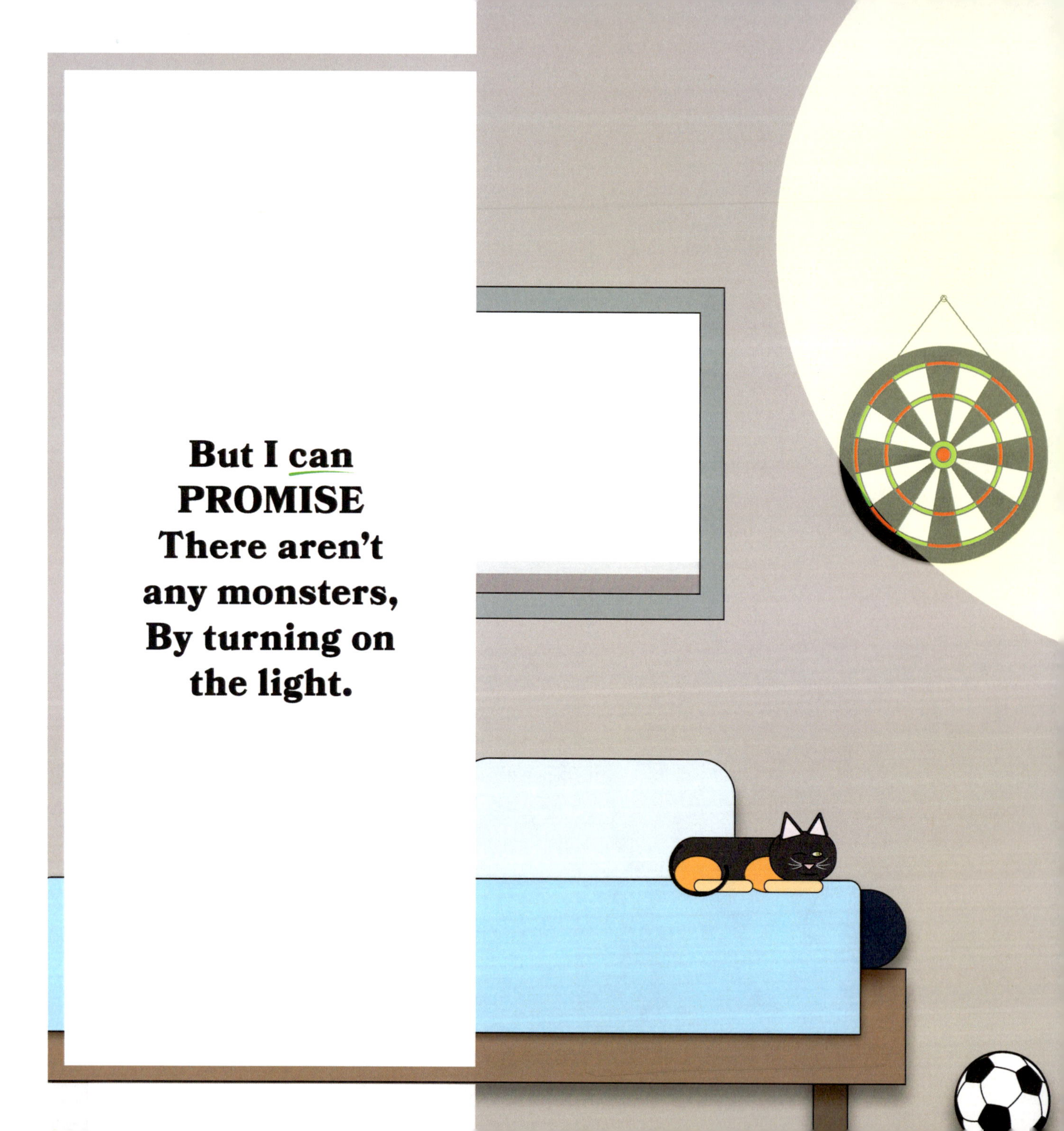

But I can
PROMISE
There aren't
any monsters,
By turning on
the light.

I can't
PROMISE
Your heart won't
hurt,
When a friend
takes your
favorite toy...

But I can <u>can</u>
PROMISE
To teach you to
share,
Which will fill
your heart with
joy.

**I can't
PROMISE
You won't make
mistakes,
Or color outside
of the lines...**

**But I can
PROMISE**
**It's okay to laugh
at them,
And show your
crooked smile.**

I can't
PROMISE
You won't scrape
your knee,
When learning to
ride a bike...

**But I can
PROMISE
To pick you up,
And encourage
you to try it
twice.**

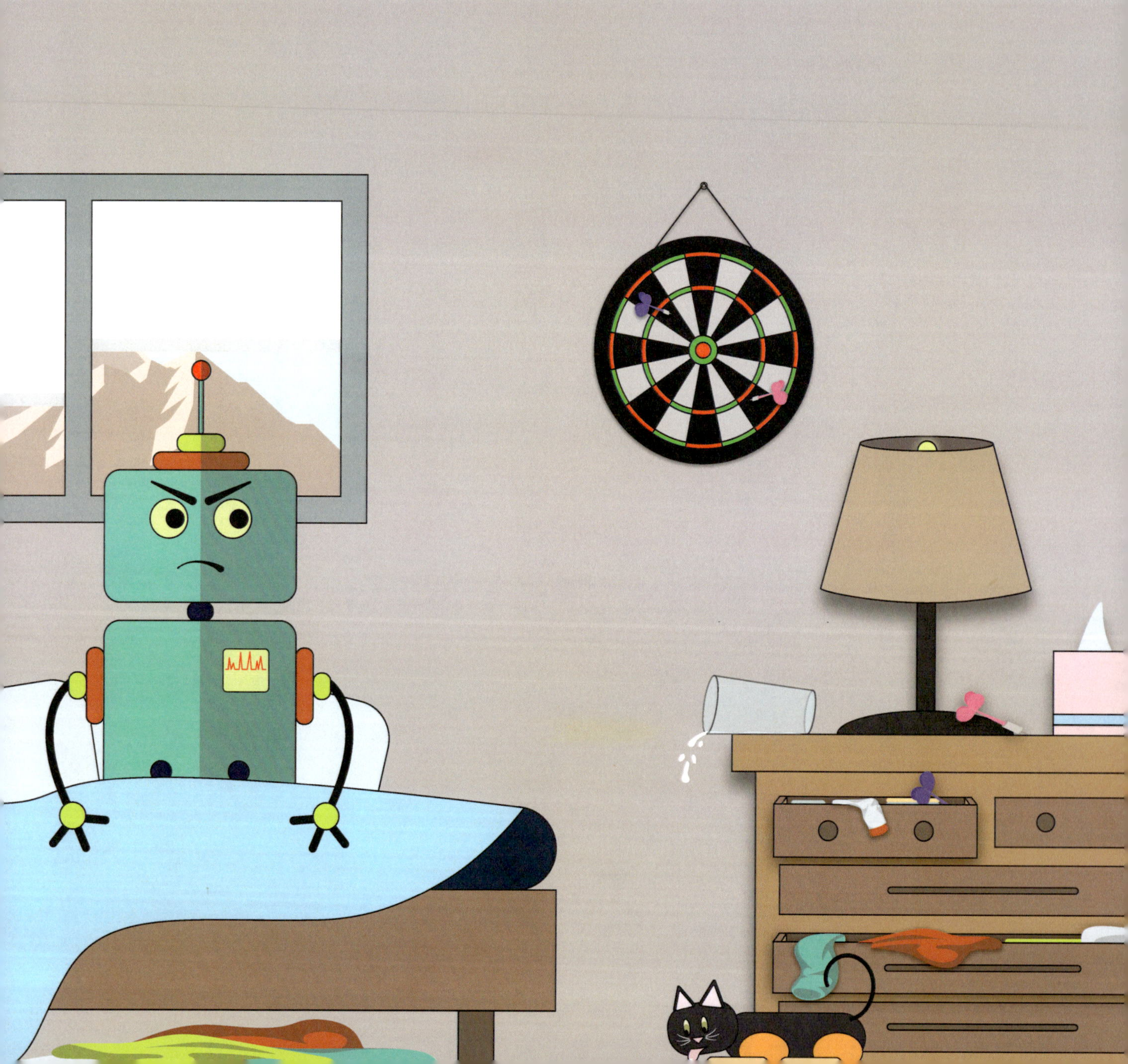

I can't <u>PROMISE</u>
PROMISE
You will always
be happy,
Or like every
decision that I
make...

But I can
PROMISE
To always listen,
And teach you to
do the same.

I am your
Protector,
And I
PROMISE
to do the best
that I can...

But part of life is
learning,
And I
PROMISE
to catch you...
Wherever you
may land.

www.ingramcontent.com/pod-product-compliance
Lightning Source LLC
Chambersburg PA
CBRC090518160726
48196CB00091B/740